HOW IS IT N
SYRuP

by R.J. Bailey

pogo

Ideas for Parents and Teachers

Pogo Books let children practice reading informational text while introducing them to nonfiction features such as headings, labels, sidebars, maps, and diagrams, as well as a table of contents, glossary, and index.

Carefully leveled text with a strong photo match offers early fluent readers the support they need to succeed.

Before Reading

- "Walk" through the book and point out the various nonfiction features. Ask the student what purpose each feature serves.
- Look at the glossary together. Read and discuss the words.

Read the Book

- Have the child read the book independently.
- Invite him or her to list questions that arise from reading.

After Reading

- Discuss the child's questions. Talk about how he or she might find answers to those questions.
- Prompt the child to think more. Ask: Syrup is made from sap, which comes from trees. Can you think of other foods you eat that come from trees?

Pogo Books are published by Jump!
5357 Penn Avenue South
Minneapolis, MN 55419
www.jumplibrary.com

Library of Congress Cataloging-in-Publication Data

Names: Bailey, R.J., author.
Title: Syrup / by R.J. Bailey.
Description: Minneapolis, MN: Jump!, Inc., [2017]
Series: How is it made? | Audience: Ages 7-10.
Includes bibliographical references and index.
Identifiers: LCCN 2016041482 (print)
LCCN 2016046903 (ebook)
ISBN 9781620315712 (hard cover: alk. paper)
ISBN 9781620316115 (pbk.)
ISBN 9781624965197 (e-book)
Subjects: LCSH: Maple syrup—Juvenile literature.
Sugar Maple—Tapping—Juvenile literature.
Classification: LCC TP395 .B35 2017 (print)
LCC TP395 (ebook) | DDC 664/.132—dc23
LC record available at https://lccn.loc.gov/2016041482

Editor: Kirsten Chang
Designer: Leah Sanders
Photo Researcher: Leah Sanders

Photo Credits: All photos by Shutterstock except: Alamy, 8, 14, 15, 16-17; Getty, 4, 6-7, 18-19; 123RF, cover.

Printed in the United States of America at Corporate Graphics in North Mankato, Minnesota.

TABLE OF CONTENTS

CHAPTER 1

STICKY AND SWEET

It's breakfast time. Yum! Pancakes! No stack is complete without a drizzle of maple syrup.

maple tree

Did you know this sweet, sticky treat comes from trees? It is made from the **sap** of maple trees. How does syrup get from a tree to a bottle? Let's find out!

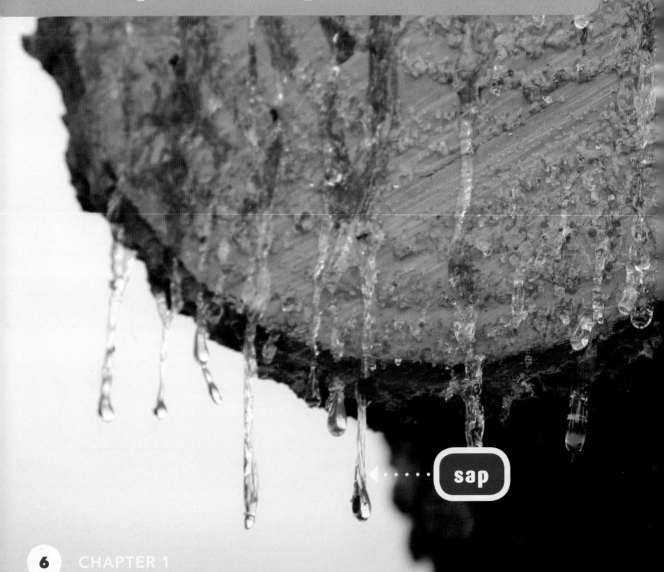

If you cut into a maple tree in late winter, sap comes out. It looks like water.

What does sap do? It carries water, sugar, and other **nutrients** to different parts of a maple tree. It keeps the tree healthy.

sap

WHERE DOES IT COME FROM?

Most maple syrup comes from sugar maple trees in North America.

■ = Sugar Maple Tree Region

N
W ┼ E
S

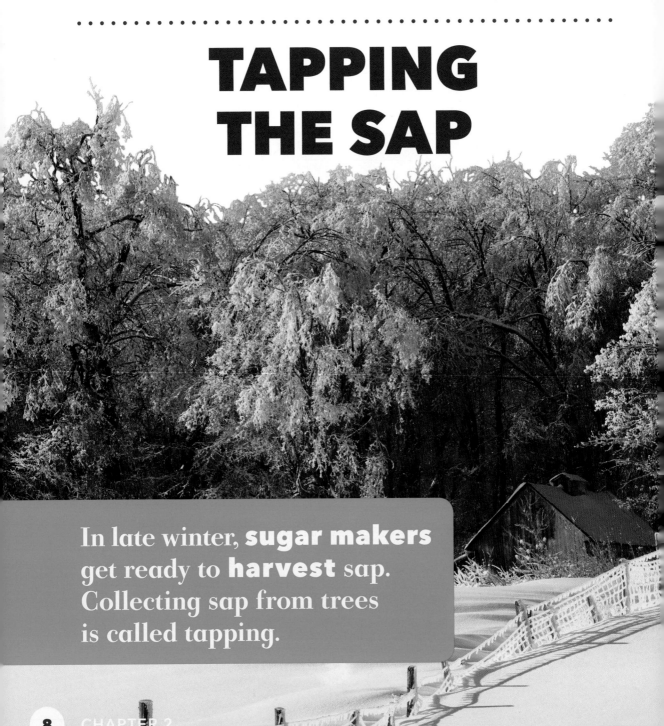

CHAPTER 2

TAPPING THE SAP

In late winter, **sugar makers** get ready to **harvest** sap. Collecting sap from trees is called tapping.

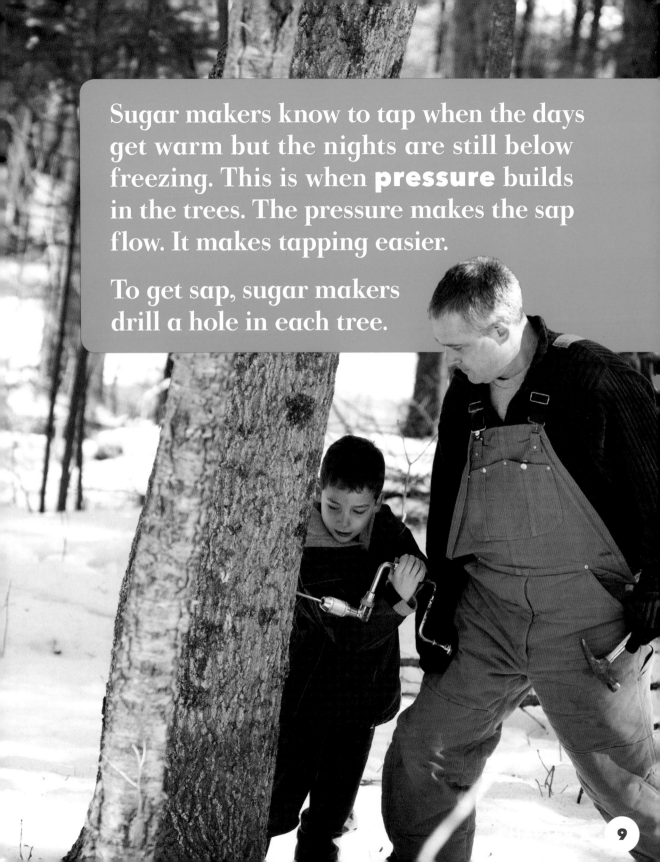

Sugar makers know to tap when the days get warm but the nights are still below freezing. This is when **pressure** builds in the trees. The pressure makes the sap flow. It makes tapping easier.

To get sap, sugar makers drill a hole in each tree.

spout

They put a tube or a **spout** with an attached bucket into the hole. Each tap produces an average of 10 gallons (38 liters) of sap.

DID YOU KNOW?

Red squirrels harvest sap, too! They scratch the tree bark. Sap comes out. After it dries, they eat it. It gives them energy during the winter.

Only a healthy tree that is 10 inches (25 centimeters) or more in **diameter** can be tapped. It usually takes 40 years for a maple tree to reach the right size.

DID YOU KNOW?

It takes about 40 gallons (151 liters) of sap to make 1 gallon (3.8 liters) of syrup.

CHAPTER 3

FROM SAP TO SYRUP

After harvesting, the sap goes to a **sugarhouse**.

SWEET MAPLES SUGARHOUSE

evaporator

The sap is boiled in a large, open pan called an **evaporator**. As it boils, the watery part of the sap evaporates.

The sap turns golden as it boils. It gets thicker and sweeter. It turns into syrup. The sugar maker opens a **valve** on the pan. The syrup comes out.

DID YOU KNOW?

Sap is about 98 percent water and 2 percent sugar. Syrup is about 33 percent water and 67 percent sugar.

The syrup is **filtered**. Tiny particles called "sugar sand" are removed. Sugar sand is harmless. But it would affect how syrup looks and tastes.

The syrup is bottled. It is **graded** by color and taste. The darker the color of the syrup, the stronger the maple flavor will be.

Then it is shipped to stores. It is ready to pour on your pancakes. Yum!

TAKE A LOOK!

How does sap become syrup?

Tapping

Filtering

Boiling

Bottling

TRY THIS!

SYRUP SNOW CANDY

Maple syrup candy is delicious! It's fun to make in winter when there is fresh snow on the ground.

What You Need:
- clean, fresh snow
- a pie pan
- ¼ cup pure maple syrup
- two popsicle sticks
- a small pot
- candy thermometer

1. Fill a pie pan with fresh, packed snow. Put it in the freezer.

2. Have an adult help you. Pour pure maple syrup into the pot. Heat until the syrup bubbles. That means it is boiling.

3. Put the candy thermometer in the syrup. Continue to boil until the thermometer reads 240 degrees Fahrenheit (115 degrees Celsius).

4. Get your pan of snow from the freezer.

5. Take the pot off the heat. Be careful! The syrup is hot. Pour the syrup in two lines on the snow.

6. Press a popsicle stick into each line of syrup. As the hot syrup cools on the cold snow, it will start to get hard. Roll the syrup up around the stick. Enjoy your syrup treat!

GLOSSARY

diameter: The distance through the center of something from one side to the other.

evaporator: An open pan that is placed over a heat source to boil sap.

filtered: Passed through a device to separate out unwanted matter.

graded: Separated and arranged by kind or class.

harvest: To gather crops.

nutrients: Substances that are essential for living things to survive and grow.

pressure: Force caused by one thing pushing against another.

sap: A watery liquid that moves through a tree and carries nutrients.

spout: A tube, pipe, or hole through which something comes out.

sugar makers: People who tap maple sap and make maple syrup.

sugarhouse: A building where maple sap is boiled and maple syrup is made.

valve: A tool that controls the flow of liquid by opening and closing.

INDEX

TO LEARN MORE

Learning more is as easy as 1, 2, 3.

1) Go to www.factsurfer.com

2) Enter "syrup" into the search box.

3) Click the "Surf" button to see a list of websites.

With factsurfer, finding more information is just a click away.